Learn to Embroider
with the Best of Leisure Arts

A fun introduction to embroidery, this book gives an overview of the tools and supplies you need, a gallery of popular stitches, and a dozen projects to practice what you learn in various styles, from redwork to crazy quilt embroidery.

8

10

12

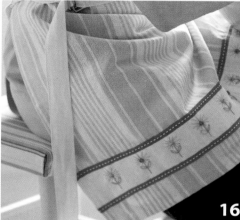

14

16

18

20

22

24

26

28

LEISURE ARTS, INC. • Little Rock, Arkansas

Getting Started

Before you begin, read through the following pages to familiarize yourself with the tools and supplies you will be using. Try your hand at making the Basic Stitches on page 5 and then get started with the beginner-friendly Soar Pincushion on page 8. As you continue learning, check out the additional stitches on pages 6-7 and 31.

Fabric

From delicate baby clothing to rough-and-tumble denim, almost any fabric is suitable for embroidery. For most beginner projects of traditional embroidery, a tightly woven, light- to medium-weight fabric is preferred. Light-colored solids or tone-on-tone prints usually work best, but subtle stripes or prints can also be used.

Thread

Thread choices for embroidery include six-strand cotton embroidery floss, over-dyed or hand-dyed six- or three-strand cotton embroidery floss, Sulky® 12wt. cotton thread, or size 8 pearl cotton.

Note: Some colors of floss, particularly reds, are not always colorfast and may bleed when washing a finished project. See Setting Color, page 3, for instructions on pre-washing to set floss color. Setting color is not recommended for hand-dyed or over-dyed floss.

Six-strand embroidery floss is usually separated into individual strands for stitching. Project instructions will usually indicate the number of strands to use. If not, experiment to determine what looks best to you.

Three-strand embroidery floss, Sulky® cotton thread, and pearl cotton are used straight off the spools and do not need to be separated.

To see which look you like best, you might want to work a small sample piece using various strands of floss or sizes of thread or pearl cotton before beginning your project.

Setting Color

1. Fill a shallow glass or plastic container half-full of cold water. Add 2 tablespoons of white vinegar; mix well.
2. Working with only one color at a time, immerse floss in mixture for 1-2 minutes.
3. Remove floss from container and rinse thoroughly under cold running water.
4. Blot thread with an old, light-colored clean towel, and allow it to dry. If color transfers to the towel during blotting, repeat rinsing and blotting until bleeding stops. If bleeding does not stop, you might want to choose a different color floss or type of thread.

Note: If a finished project must be washed, always use cold water and a dry iron. Using hot water or steam may re-activate some dyes and cause bleeding.

Needles

Needles are a very personal choice. A sharp point is necessary to pierce the fabric, but the size and type of the needle is up to you. Quilting betweens (size 8 or 10) are short, sharp needles, while embroidery needles (size 8 or 10) are longer.

Look for needles that have eyes large enough to accommodate the number of strands or size thread you will be using without making excessively large holes in the fabric.

Try different sizes and styles of needles until you find one that suits you.

Hoop

It is important to keep the fabric stretched tightly while embroidering. Many stitchers prefer wooden hoops. Choose a hoop that will allow you to stitch all or most of the design before repositioning the fabric.

Other Tools

A needle threader comes in handy when using multiple strands of floss, while a needlecase safely stores your needles when not in use.

A thimble protects the middle finger while embroidering, but it can take some getting used to.

Small, sharp embroidery scissors clip thread and floss quickly and neatly. Protect the points (and your fingers!) by storing the scissors in a sheath.

Sizing Patterns

Patterns for the projects in this book are printed at the exact size needed, unless otherwise noted. If you wish to change the size of a pattern, for example, to make a different size pillow or to make a design fit in a particular frame, divide the desired height of the pattern by the actual height of the pattern. Multiply the result by 100 and photocopy the pattern at this percentage.

For example, you want to enlarge the pattern to $11\frac{1}{2}$" high and the printed pattern is 10" high.
$11\frac{1}{2} \div 10 = 1.15$
$1.15 \times 100 = 115\%$
Copy the pattern at 115%

Or, to make the pattern smaller, say $7\frac{1}{2}$" high, use the same formula.
$7\frac{1}{2} \div 10 = .75$
$.75 \times 100 = 75\%$
Copy the pattern at 75%

Transferring Designs

To transfer designs from the book to fabric, choose one of the following methods. *Note:* It is not necessary to transfer all details of each stitch. For example, when transferring Blanket Stitches, you can draw a single line or simply refer to the project's Embroidery Diagram for placement.

Direct Tracing

- Fine-point water- or air-soluble pen
- tape
- light source

Tape the fabric piece over the pattern and trace the design with a fine-point water- or air-soluble pen. If you have trouble seeing through the fabric, make a copy of the pattern. Tape the copy to a sunny window, place the fabric over the copy and trace the design. A light box or a glass-top table with a lamp under it will work as well.

Freezer Paper Tracing

- Freezer paper (8½" x 11" sheets)
- copier/printer
- light source
- Fine-point water- or air-soluble pen

The freezer paper method stabilizes the fabric pieces which makes tracing easier. Using the mirror image function on a copier, copy the pattern onto the paper side of freezer paper. Larger patterns may have to be copied in sections and joined. With shiny side down, iron the freezer paper to the wrong side of your fabric piece. Using a sunny window or light box, trace the design with a fine-point water- or air-soluble pen. Remove freezer paper before stitching.

Transfer Paper

- tissue paper
- wax-free transfer paper

Trace the pattern onto tissue paper. Place the transfer paper, colored side down, between the fabric and the pattern. Use a pen to draw over the design. Embroider the design.

Transfer-Eze™

- Transfer-Eze™ transfer paper
- inkjet printer

Transfer-Eze™ is a pliable film through which you can embroider. Photocopy the design onto the "film" side of a Transfer-Eze sheet using the light setting on your ink jet printer. Larger patterns may have to be copied in sections and joined. Remove the paper backing and adhere the pattern to the right side of the fabric. Embroider the design. Trim the excess Transfer-Eze film away from the embroidery. Soak the fabric in cold water to dissolve the remaining film.

Embroidering

1. Place the traced fabric piece, right side up, in a hoop; smooth any wrinkles. It will be easier to embroider if the fabric is stretched tightly in the hoop.
2. Cut an 18"-24" length of floss, pearl cotton, or thread. Longer lengths tend to twist, look worn, and knot easier. Thread a needle with the desired number of strands and knot one end.
3. Following your project's Embroidery Diagram, work indicated stitches over all lines of the design.
4. If you used direct tracing or freezer paper tracing, remove any visible marks with a damp cotton swab. If you used Transfer-Eze, follow manufacturer's instructions to remove film. Place the piece, embroidered side down, on a white or light-colored fluffy towel and press.

Basic Stitches

Here are some of the most widely used embroidery stitches. Follow the stitch diagrams to bring the needle up at odd numbers and down at even numbers.

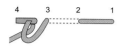

Running Stitch

Make a series of straight stitches over and under the fabric, keeping the stitches the same size and using equal spacing.

Backstitch

Forming a continuous line, Backstitches can be made in straight or curved lines. The stitches can be any size but should be uniform in length.

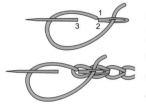

Chain Stitch

Be sure to keep the loop of working thread below the point of the needle as you make each chain link, and take care to maintain even tension. Secure the final loop with a small straight stitch.

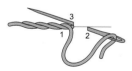

Stem Stitch

Keeping the working thread below the stitching line, make your stitches short and even in length. Whether straight or curved, the finished line should resemble a rope.

Straight Stitch

This simple, versatile stitch can be made in any length and at any angle as needed.

Satin Stitch

Stitches should be placed side by side, touching but not overlapping. Practice will help you achieve a smooth appearance and even edges. Avoid making the stitches too long; to fill large areas, consider using Long and Short Satin Stitch (page 7).

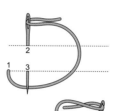

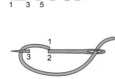

Blanket Stitch

Strive to make uniformly sized stitches with even spacing. It may be helpful to use your thumb to pull the working thread into a loop below the point of the needle. Blanket Stitch can be worked along an edge or on the surface of the fabric.

Lazy Daisy Stitch

Often used for flower petals, this stitch is like one link of the Chain Stitch. Working the petals in a circle creates a flower shape (see page 31); the center can be accented with a French Knot or a bead or button.

French Knot

The key to neat knots is to wrap the thread around the needle only once and to hold the thumb of your free hand on the knot while pulling the thread through to complete the stitch. For larger knots, use more strands of thread.

Stitch Gallery

These embroidery stitches will let you develop your repertoire beyond the basics given on page 5.
Follow the stitch diagrams to bring the needle up at odd numbers and down at even numbers.

Blanket Stitch – Long and Short

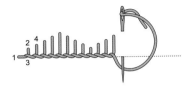

Blanket Stitch – Variation

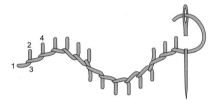

Bullion Knot

Buttonhole Stitch

Buttonhole Wheel

Chain Stitch – Zigzag

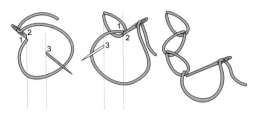

Couching Stitch

Cretan Stitch – Closed

Cross Stitch

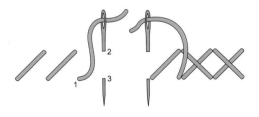

Cross Stitch – Double

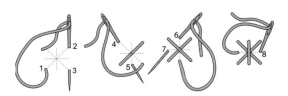

Feather Stitch

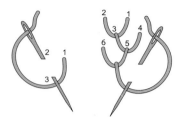

Fly Stitch

Herringbone Stitch

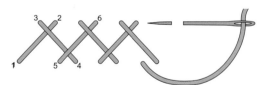

Herringbone Stitch – Closed

Satin Stitch – Long and Short

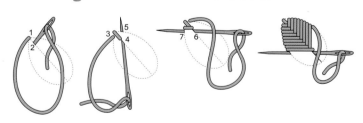

Satin Stitch – Padded

Begin with
Split Stitch
outline →

Seeding

Sheaf Stitch

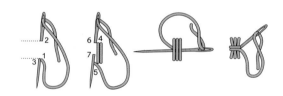

Spider Web

Split Stitch

For crazy quilt embroidery stitches, see page 31.

Beginner Basics

Chain Stitch, Stem Stitch, and other stitches that form outlines are some of the basics that most embroiderers learn as beginners. They are very easy to do and very versatile, being appropriate for creating straight or curved lines. Try your hand with this sweet bird design, finished as a pincushion. All the stitches it uses are explained on page 5.

SOAR PINCUSHION
Designed by Kathy Schmitz.

Finished Size:
Approximately 3¹/₂" x 6"

Supplies
Before beginning your project, please read Getting Started, pages 2-4, to choose a transfer method and learn about any additional supplies needed.

- 8" x 10" rectangle of tan tone-on-tone fabric
- 6" x 8" rectangle of backing fabric
- Transfer supplies (varies with chosen transfer method)
- Embroidery floss in desired color (we used Weeks Dye Works #1269 Chestnut)
- Crushed walnut shells* or polyester fiberfill

* Crushed walnut shells are available in pet supply stores. In addition to being a natural, sustainable material, they contain oils that help keep needles and pins sharp and clean.

Embroidering the Pincushion

Follow Transferring Designs, page 4, to transfer the embroidery design to fabric. Follow Basic Stitches, page 5, for stitch techniques.

1. Using your preferred method, transfer embroidery design and heavy outer cutting line from pattern, opposite, to tone-on-tone rectangle. Transfer cutting line only to backing fabric rectangle.
2. Embroider the transferred design following the embroidery diagram, opposite.

Assembling the Pincushion

Match right sides and use ¹/₄" seam allowances throughout.

1. Following cutting line, cut pincushion top from embroidered rectangle and pincushion bottom from backing rectangle.
2. Leaving an opening for turning, sew pincushion top and bottom together. Clip curves; turn pincushion right side out.
3. Fill pincushion with crushed walnut shells or polyester fiberfill; hand stitch opening closed.

EMBROIDERY KEY
Use 2 strands of floss.

L Blanket Stitch	/ Running Stitch
/ Chain Stitch	/ Stem Stitch
• French Knot	/ Straight Stitch

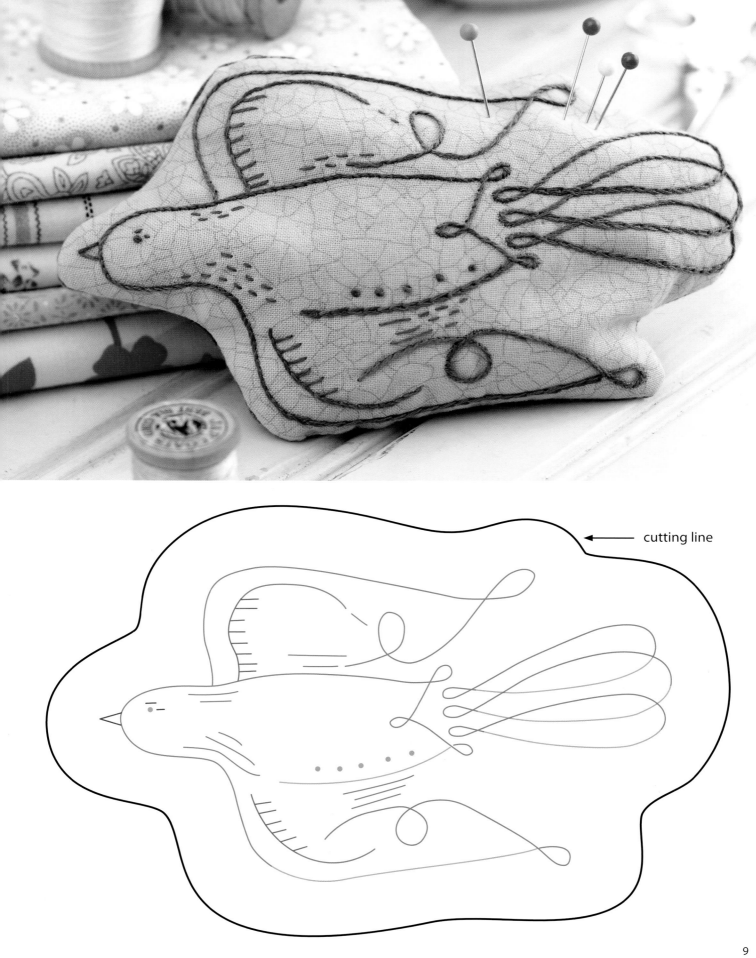

cutting line

Simple Redwork

One of the simplest types of embroidery you can learn is old-timey redwork. You can stitch the design all in traditional red floss or update it with bright color combinations that show off the creative potential of easy Running Stitch, Backstitch, and a few others. You'll be delighted by how quickly these designs come to life, whether you choose Love My Cat or the bonus design, Teddy Bear Love.

LOVE MY CAT

Designed by Holly Witt.

Finished Size:

Approx. 4" x 6"

Supplies

- Red embroidery floss
- Precut mat (8" x 10" with opening of $4^{1}/_{2}$" x $6^{1}/_{2}$")
- Fabric to cover mat
- Fabric for bow
- Frame ($11^{3}/_{4}$" x $14^{3}/_{4}$" with $7^{1}/_{2}$" x $9^{1}/_{2}$" opening)
- Paper-backed fusible web
- Four $^{3}/_{4}$" buttons
- White poster board
- Fabric marking pen
- Spray adhesive
- Hot glue gun
- Transfer supplies (see page 4)

Embroidering the Design

Follow Transferring Designs, page 4, to transfer the embroidery design, opposite, to fabric. Follow Basic Stitches, page 5, for stitch techniques.

Finishing

1. Follow manufacturer's instructions to fuse web to wrong side of design. Fuse design to poster board; trim poster board to fit in frame.
2. To cover frame front, use fabric marking pen to draw around precut mat and mat opening on wrong side of fabric. Cutting 1" outside drawn lines, cut out shape and opening. Clip fabric at corners of opening.
3. Apply spray adhesive to precut mat. Center mat on wrong side of fabric. Fold fabric edges at opening of mat and on sides to back; glue in place.
4. Place mat, then design in frame; secure in place.
5. Use floss to sew through buttons; glue buttons to mat.
6. Tear a 2" strip of fabric. Tie fabric strip into bow; glue to frame.

Love My Cat

BONUS DESIGN:
Teddy Bear Love

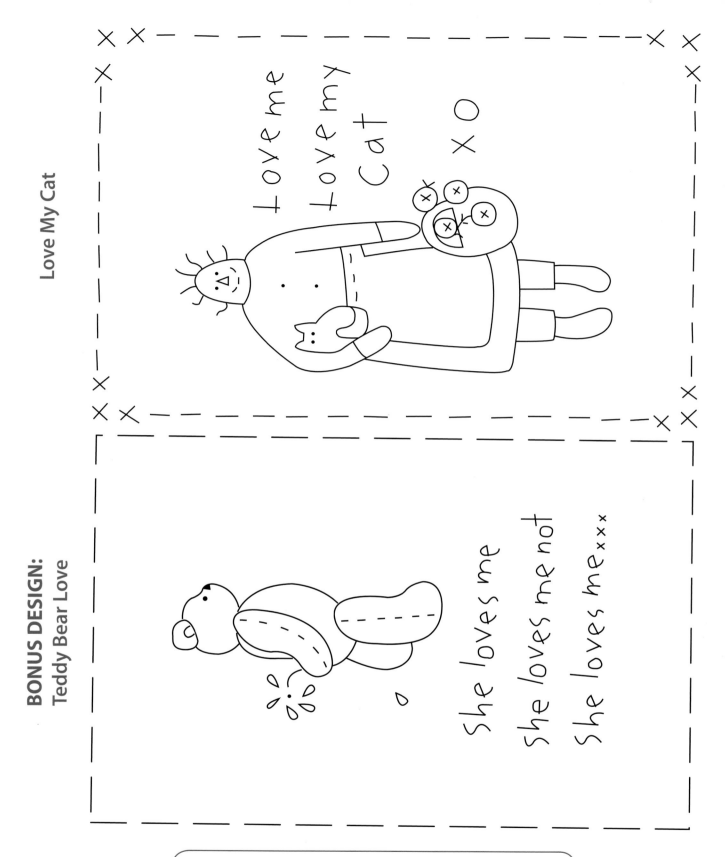

EMBROIDERY KEY
Use 2 strands of floss.

— Backstitch	× Cross Stitch	◠ Lazy Daisy
- - - Running Stitch	● French Knot	

Modern Primitive

Translate any image into a simple line drawing and you've got a pattern for primitive embroidery – then modernize it with today's hottest colors. The casual style of these designs makes them a good choice for beginners, because any imperfections will just add to their charm!

EACH DAY
Designed by Jennie Baer.

Finished Size:
Approx. 3" x 7¾" plus desired margin on all sides

Supplies
- Transfer supplies (see page 4)
- Cream linen (we cut a 9½" x 15" piece)
- Embroidery floss (see Embroidery Key)
- Blue colored pencil (optional)
- Frame (ours has a 5¼" x 10½" opening)

Embroidering the Design
Follow Transferring Designs, page 4, to transfer the embroidery design to fabric. Follow Basic Stitches, page 5, for stitch techniques. Transfer the pattern and embroider the design on the linen piece. Notice that the Satin Stitch flower petals and heart are edged with Stem Stitch or Backstitch for a smooth finish.

Finishing
To soften the look, we lightly shaded the jar with a blue pencil (to add shading to yours, first practice on a linen scrap until you get the hang of it). To finish the stitched piece, we liked the simplicity of this red frame.

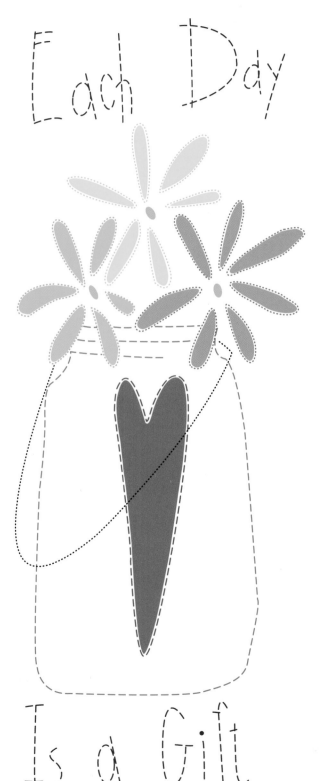

EMBROIDERY KEY

Satin Stitch – 3 strands
- DMC 347
- DMC 472
- DMC 721
- DMC 743
- DMC 3832

Stem Stitch
- DMC 721 – 2 strands
- DMC 743 – 2 strands
- DMC 839 – 3 strands
- DMC 3832 – 2 strands

Backstitch
- DMC 347 – 2 strands
- DMC 347 – 3 strands
- DMC 3766 – 3 strands

French Knot – 3 strands
- DMC 347

Each Day

Is a Gift

Traditional

To try your hand at traditional embroidery, check out this pretty floral design with flowing vines and words of wisdom. Depending on the size of your project, add texture with fibers beyond the usual embroidery floss, such as pearl cotton or fine yarns. Felted wool makes a soft background for this lustrous stitchery.

ALL WE NEED

Finished Size:
Approx. 10" x 12" plus desired margin on all sides

Supplies
- Tissue paper and straight pins
- Hand-dyed wool (we used a 13" x 16" piece)
- Embroidery floss (see Embroidery Key)
- Pearl cotton (see Embroidery Key)
- Wood frame (ours has a 10½" x 13½" opening)

Embroidering the Design
Use a photocopier to enlarge the pattern, opposite, by 140 percent. Trace the enlarged pattern onto tissue paper and pin it to the fabric. Embroider the design, stitching through the tissue paper. Follow Basic Stitches, page 5, for stitch techniques. When you are finished, carefully tear away the tissue paper.

Finishing
We framed our design in a rustic wood frame.

DMC COLORS

■ 335 Dk Pink	■ 704 Lime Green
■ 347 Dk Coral	■ 818 Lt Pink
■ 350 Coral	■ 957 Pink
■ 352 Lt Coral	■ 966 Lt Green
■ 367 Dk Green	■ 3822 Gold

EMBROIDERY KEY
Use 6 strands of embroidery floss for French Knots and 1 strand of pearl cotton for all other stitching.

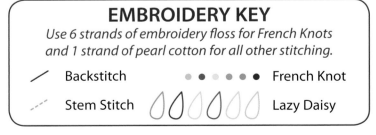

Backstitch   • • • • • French Knot

Stem Stitch   Lazy Daisy

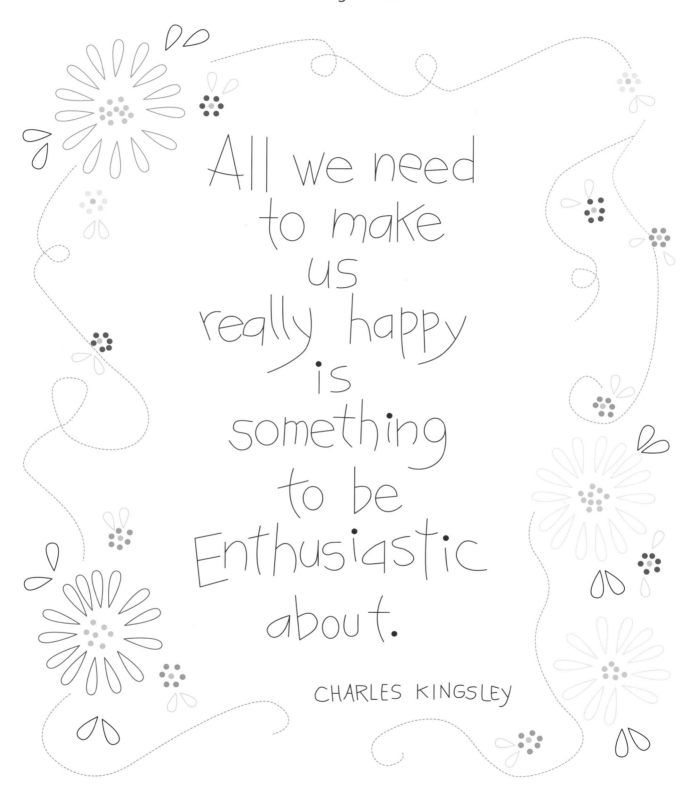

All we need
to make
us
really happy
is
something
to be
Enthusiastic
about.

CHARLES KINGSLEY

Little Touches

One of the great things about embroidery is that it only takes a touch of it to add a lot of charm to an item. This Tea Towel Apron is a wonderful example. You simply repeat the easy flower motif across the front and use buttons for the center of each bloom. You could stitch directly on the tea towel, but we stitched on an add-on fabric strip so we could hide the back of our work.

TEA TOWEL APRON

Finished Size:

Approx. 16$\frac{1}{2}$" x 24$\frac{1}{2}$"

Supplies

- Transfer supplies (see page 4)
- Cream fabric (cut a strip 5" x 25" or $\frac{1}{2}$" longer than the length of the tea towel)
- Tea towel (we trimmed ours and hemmed it to 16$\frac{1}{2}$" x 24$\frac{1}{2}$")
- Embroidery floss (see Embroidery Key)
- $\frac{1}{4}$" diameter buttons
- $\frac{3}{8}$" wide ribbon
- clear monofilament thread
- 1$\frac{1}{4}$" wide twill tape (cut tape 1 yard longer than waist measurement)
- two 1" wide rectangular rings

Embroidering the Design

Follow Transferring Designs, page 4, to center and transfer the embroidery design, right, to the fabric strip. (We repeated the design to transfer 11 flowers across the strip.) Embroider the motifs, following Basic Stitches, page 5, for stitch techniques. Add button flower centers. Trim the strip to 2$\frac{1}{2}$" wide. Press the short ends $\frac{1}{4}$" to the wrong side and pin the strip to the towel.

Cover the long edges of the strip with ribbon and machine zigzag stitch it to the towel with clear thread.

Finishing

For the apron belt, press one end of the twill tape $\frac{1}{2}$" to the wrong side. Fold the tape about 7" from the pressed end and slide the rings on the tape to the fold. Sew across the tape to hold the rings in place.

Beginning with the pressed end at the top left corner of the towel, pin the tape along the top edge and topstitch, sewing across the tape $\frac{1}{4}$" from each side of the ring seam.

Add a twill tape belt loop near the left edge of the belt. Try on the apron. Trim and hem the loose end of the belt.

EMBROIDERY KEY

Use 6 strands of floss.

- Straight Stitch
- Lazy Daisy
- Button Placement

Appliqué

Embroidery is often used to embellish appliquéd designs, either to conceal or accent the edges, or to add features such as the faces on our cute apple and orange. With their rickrack trim, these dishtowels offer cozy, vintage style.

APPLIQUÉD DISHTOWELS

Finished Size:
Apple approx. 4¹/₂" x 4¹/₂"
Orange approx. 4³/₄" x 3³/₄"

Supplies

- Dishtowels (we used 2 green and white striped towels)
- Fabric scraps (we used orange solid and red mini check fabrics)
- Red jumbo rickrack (to determine length needed, measure width of dishtowel and add 1"
- Red embroidery floss
- Paper-backed fusible web
- Tissue paper
- Clear monofilament thread (optional)
- Water-soluble fabric pen

Applique

For each appliqué piece, you will need to reverse the pattern. To make a reversed pattern, trace appliqué shape onto tissue paper; turn tissue paper over and re-trace the drawn lines. Trace this reversed pattern onto the paper-side of fusible web.

Rough cut piece from web approximately ¹/₄" outside drawn lines. Follow manufacturer's instructions to fuse web piece to wrong side of fabric. Cut out piece along outer drawn lines (including arms and legs). Remove paper backing and fuse piece to dishtowel. Use water-soluble pen to transfer embroidery details.

To make your appliqué more durable, you may choose to machine zigzag stitch all raw edges of the appliqué using clear monofilament thread in the machine needle and general all-purpose thread in the bobbin.

Embroidering Each Design
Embroider, following Basic Stitches, page 5, for stitch techniques.

Finishing
Referring to photo for placement and folding ends of rickrack to back of towel, topstitch rickrack across width of towel.

EMBROIDERY KEY
Use 3 strands of floss for Stem Stitches; use 2 strands for Running Stitches and Straight Stitches.

/ ╱ Running Stitch (varying stitch length)

/ ╱ Stem Stitch

/ Straight Stitch

EMBROIDERY KEY

Use 3 strands of floss for Stem Stitches and French Knots; use 2 strands for Straight Stitches.

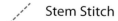 Stem Stitch

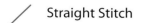 Straight Stitch

• French Knot

Retro

Adding embroidered motifs to blue jeans is a favorite retro technique, especially when you use Sixties-style motifs such as this giant paisley design. But we couldn't resist showing you how the same design looks elegant when used on a fancy pillow. Whatever type of project you choose, your embellishment will turn the ordinary into the extraordinary!

BLUE JEANS
Designed by Patti Wallenfang.

Finished Size:
Approx. 5½" x 7¼"

Supplies
- Transfer supplies (see page 4)
- Blue jeans
- Embroidery floss (see Embroidery Key)

Embroidering the Design
Follow Transferring Designs, page 4, to transfer the embroidery design to blue jeans. Follow Basic Stitches, page 5, for stitch techniques. Notice that the Satin Stitch scallops are edged with Stem Stitch for a smooth finish.

OPTION:
For a totally different look, change floss colors and embroider the design on a fancy pillow. Using 3 strands of floss, we chose a gold and 2 browns: DMC 729, 3826, and 838.

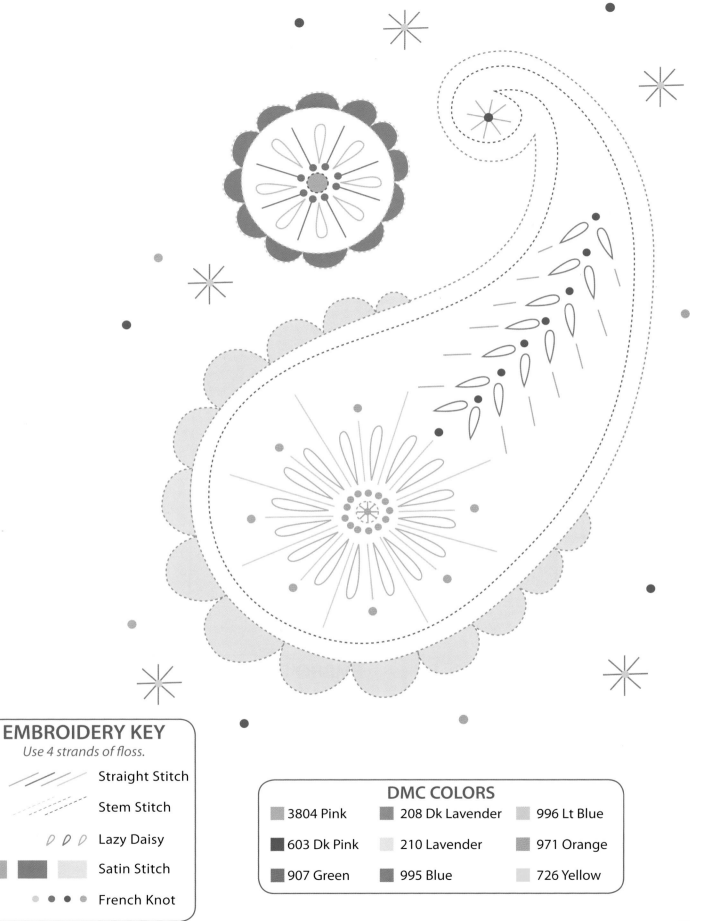

EMBROIDERY KEY
Use 4 strands of floss.

Straight Stitch

Stem Stitch

Lazy Daisy

Satin Stitch

French Knot

DMC COLORS

3804 Pink	208 Dk Lavender	996 Lt Blue
603 Dk Pink	210 Lavender	971 Orange
907 Green	995 Blue	726 Yellow

Fashion

Whether it is for the quintessential denim jacket or a romantic blouse, embroidery makes a beautiful addition to clothing of all kinds. Take inspiration from the high-dollar fashions you see celebrities wearing and make it yourself for a song. The sky is the limit!

DAISY JACKET

Designed by Patti Wallenfang.

Supplies
- Transfer supplies (see page 4)
- Denim jacket
- Embroidery floss (see Embroidery Key)

Embroidering the Design
Follow Transferring Designs, page 4, to transfer the embroidery design to jacket. Follow stitch diagrams on pages 5-7 for stitch techniques. Notice that the Lazy Daisy Stitches are elongated and that the Satin Stitch leaves are edged with Stem Stitch and detailed with Straight Stitch.

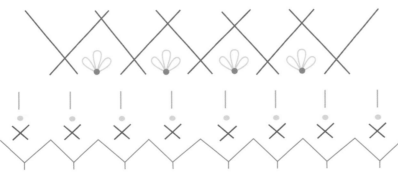

DMC COLORS
- 701 Green
- 703 Lt Green
- 740 Orange
- 725 Gold
- 434 Brown

EMBROIDERY KEY
Use 4 strands of floss.

- Straight Stitch
- Stem Stitch
- Lazy Daisy
- Herringbone Stitch
- French Knot
- Fly Stitch
- Satin Stitch

For Babies & Children

Everything for babies and children looks so much cuter with colorful pictures on it, from clothing to room accessories. This Pillowcase Dress is oh-so adorable, easily and sweetly sewn and embroidered with a kitten and a special little girl's name.

Pillowcase Dress

Finished Size:
Design approx. 5¼" x 5¼"

Supplies
- Transfer supplies (see page 4)
- 1 Standard size pillowcase
- Embroidery floss (see Embroidery Key)
- 1⅓ Yards of narrow ribbon trim
- Clear monofilament thread
- 2 Yards of ⅝" wide ribbon, cut into two equal lengths

Embroidering the Design

To make pattern for child's name, print name from computer, freehand name, or allow child to write name. (Ours is approximately 1½" high.) Follow Transferring Designs, page 4, to transfer name pattern to pillowcase above hemline. Refer to photo for placement to transfer kitten design to pillowcase.

Embroider name using Stem Stitch and 2 strands of floss. Embroider kitten design following Basic Stitches, page 5, for stitch techniques. Notice that the Satin Stitch areas of eyes and nose are edged with Stem Stitch. The Lazy Daisy Stitches are used only on the kitten's apron, not in the flowers of the bouquet.

DMC COLORS
- 318 Gray
- 600 Dk Pink
- 604 Pink
- 726 Yellow
- 741 Orange
- 813 Blue
- 910 Green

Finishing

Aligning narrow ribbon trim along hemline, machine zigzag stitch trim to pillowcase using clear monofilament thread in machine needle and general all-purpose thread in bobbin.

Open the closed end of the pillowcase with a seam ripper. Fold pillowcase in half lengthwise. Measure from the top of the child's shoulder to the armpit and add 1¹/₂". Slightly curving at sides of pillowcase, cut corners for arms the determined measurement deep and 2" wide (Fig. 1).

Hem angled cuts, turning to wrong side ¹/₄" twice. Press top raw edges ¹/₄" and then 1" to wrong side for ribbon casings. Topstitch along bottom folded edge of each casing.

Attach a large safety pin at end of ribbon and thread one ribbon through each casing. Tie ribbon ends into bows at either side of neck.

Fig. 1

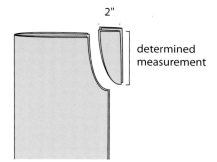

2"

determined
measurement

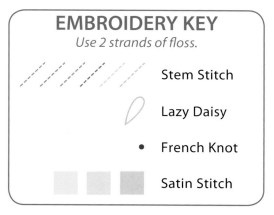

EMBROIDERY KEY
Use 2 strands of floss.

Stem Stitch

Lazy Daisy

• French Knot

Satin Stitch

Home Accessories

Embroidery is a great tool for dressing up all kinds of home accessories, from pillows and throws to curtains, framed pieces, and tablecloths. The wide range of colors available in embroidery floss, yarn, and other fibers lets you create harmony throughout your home. For a personal touch, include monograms.

Throw

Finished Size:
Monogram approx. 6" high

Supplies
- Transfer supplies (see page 4)
- Purchased cream solid throw (or 2 yards of 58" wide cream solid wool or fleece fabric)
- Embroidery floss (see Embroidery Key)
- Red 100% cotton medium weight yarn

Preparing the Throw
If using yardage, trim selvages. Hem all four sides of fabric by pressing edges to wrong side ¹/₂" (twice for wool and once for fleece) and topstitching with matching thread.

Embroidering the Design
To make pattern for monogram, photocopy desired letter, enlarging it to approximately 6" high. (You also can write the letter freehand or use your favorite font to print it from a computer.)

Referring to photo for placement, follow Transferring Designs, page 4, to transfer monogram and flowers to throw. Embroider monogram with 1 strand of cotton yarn using Stem Stitches and Satin Stitches.

Embroider flowers using 6 strands of floss and following Basic Stitches, page 5, for stitch techniques. Using cotton yarn, work Blanket Stitches around edge of throw.

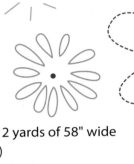

DMC COLORS

603 Pink	813 Blue	3804 Dk Pink
726 Yellow	947 Orange	

EMBROIDERY KEY
Use 1 strand of cotton yarn for monogram and 6 strands of floss for flowers.

- Chain Stitch
- Stem Stitch
- Straight Stitch
- Lazy Daisy
- French Knot
- Satin Stitch

Crazy Quilt Embroidery

Crazy quilt embroidery has been popular since the late 19th century, when quilters began using it to embellish the seams of their randomly shaped patches, as well as the patches themselves. This little pillow is a fun beginner project. We used the pattern on page 30 but simplified it by substituting buttons and bows for stitchery in some of the sections and using lace along some of the seams. To create your own precious pillow, start with scraps of six different fabrics in your favorite color scheme.

CRAZY QUILT PILLOW

Design by Patricia Eaton.

Finished Size

Approx. 6$\frac{1}{8}$" square, excluding fringe

Supplies

- Scraps of 6 coordinating cotton fabrics
- Fabric for pillow back (approx. 8" square)
- Embroidery floss in desired colors
- Lace, buttons, and other trim, as desired
- Glass seed beads in 2 colors (we used approx. 1,300 of Color A and 300 of Color B)
- Clear nylon thread
- Polyester fiberfill
- Transfer supplies (see page 30)

Instructions

1. Trace heavy lines of block pattern, page 30, onto paper. Turn paper over and re-trace lines to reverse pattern (reversed side of paper will face up when you are ready to sew).
2. Using 6 different scraps of coordinating cottons, label fabrics A-F to match sections on block pattern. Use the non-reversed paper pattern as a guide to roughly cut out one fabric piece for each area of the pattern. Pieces should be at least $\frac{1}{2}$" larger on all sides than the corresponding section on the block.
3. With non-reversed side of paper pattern facing up, center fabric piece A on section A with right side of fabric facing out. Holding fabric and pattern in front of a light source, make sure that fabric extends beyond all section A seamlines; pin in place.
4. Place fabric piece B on top of A, with right sides together. Use your light source to check that when you sew A and B pieces together along the line separating those sections, that fabric piece B will completely cover section B on the pattern when it is opened up. Once adjusted, place paper pattern, with fabric side down, under your sewing machine needle. Using a short straight stitch, sew directly on top of line separating sections A and B. Turn paper over and trim fabric seam allowance to $\frac{1}{4}$". Open fabric piece B and press; pin in place.
5. Repeat Step 4 to add remaining fabric pieces to paper pattern.
6. Using a medium stitch length, stay-stitch along outer lines of block. Trim excess fabric $\frac{1}{2}$" from edges to complete block. Tear away paper pattern.
7. Referring to photo (opposite) and pattern (page 30), embroider block for pillow front as desired. No seam-covering stitches were used in our model; lace trims were stitched along two seams.
8. For pillow back, cut a square of fabric same size as pillow front. With right sides facing, sew pillow front and back together, leaving an opening for turning. Turn pillow right side out; press. Stuff with fiberfill and sew opening closed.

9. To add beaded fringe, thread beading needle with an 18" length of nylon thread. Take several small stitches at one corner of pillow to secure thread. Thread 7 purple, 3 pink, and 1 purple seed bead onto thread. Referring to Beaded Fringe Diagram, skip last bead on thread, then thread needle back through pink beads. Thread 7 more purple beads onto thread. Take a small stitch in seamline of pillow about $3/8$" from first stitch. Continue to repeat sequence around entire edge of pillow.

Beaded Fringe Diagram

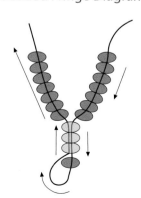

TRANSFERRING THE DESIGN TO THE BLOCK

Method 1: Make a copy of the pattern. For light-colored fabrics, use a light source, such as a light table or a window, to trace design onto fabric using a pencil.

Method 2: For dark-colored fabrics or fabrics that you don't want to risk leaving permanent marks on, trace design onto a piece of heat-sensitive brush-off fabric stabilizer or water-soluble fabric stabilizer (available at fabric stores) using a permanent fine-point pen. Baste the stabilizer onto the right side of the block. Embroider design, stitching through stabilizer. When stitching is complete, remove basting threads and stabilizer.

Include ¹/₂" seam allowance on all sides of block and each fabric section.

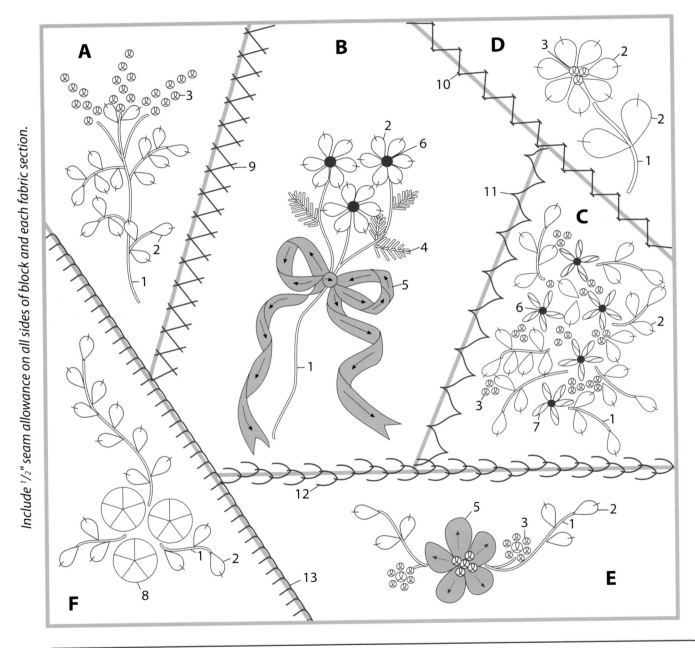

EMBROIDERY KEY

1 – Stem Stitch
2 – Lazy Daisy
3 – French Knot or Bead
4 – Fishbone Stitch
5 – Satin Stitch
6 – Bead or French Knot
7 – Wrapped Straight Stitch
8 – Woven Rose
9 – Herringbone Stitch
10 – Chevron Stitch
11 – Cretan Stitch
12 – Feather Stitch
13 – Blanket Stitch

EMBROIDERY STITCHES USED IN CRAZY QUILT PILLOW

Bring needle up at odd numbers and down at even numbers.

Blanket Stitch – Use 2 or 3 strands of floss

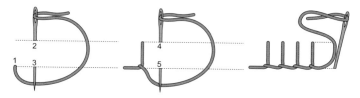

Chevron Stitch – Use 3 strands of floss

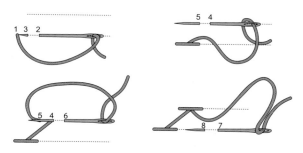

Cretan Stitch – Use 3 strands of floss

Feather Stitch – Use 2 or 3 strands of floss

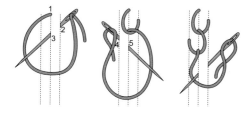

Fishbone Stitch – Use 2 or 3 strands of floss

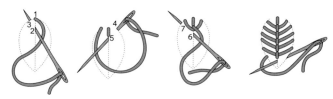

French Knot – Use 3 to 12 strands of floss

Herringbone Stitch – Use 2 or 3 strands of floss

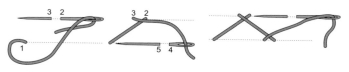

Lazy Daisy – Use 2 to 6 strands of floss

Satin Stitch – Use 2 or 3 strands of floss

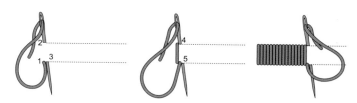

Stem Stitch – Use 2 or 3 strands of floss

Woven Rose – Use 2 strands of floss for spokes, and 6 strands of floss for weaving

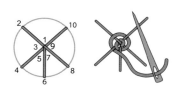

Wrapped Straight Stitch – Use 3 to 6 strands of floss

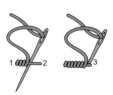

For more embroidery stitches, see pages 5-7.

Be Creative!

Combine various stitches to create your own unique look. For clarity, each stitch within one combination is shown in a different color. You can use as many or as few colors as you want.

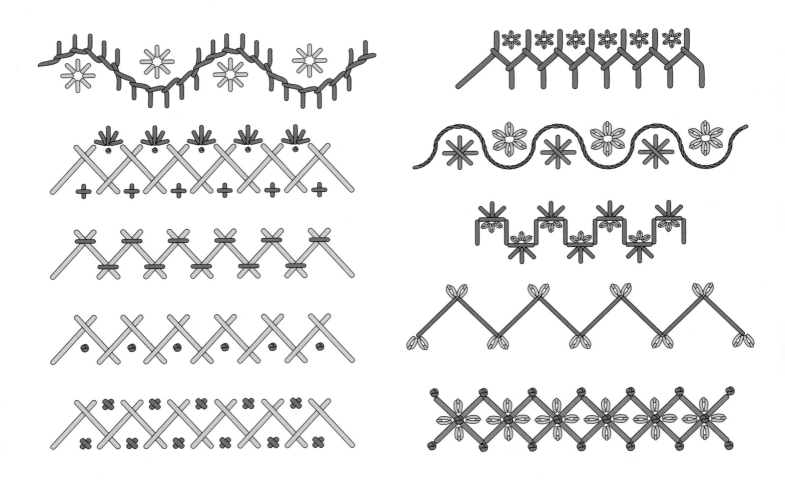

We have made every effort to ensure that these instructions are accurate and complete. We cannot, however, be responsible for human error, typographical mistakes, or variations in individual work.